Moving Toward Higher Ground

Moving Toward Higher Ground

Dr. Joël Hilaire

S&W

Steward & Wise
CHRISTIAN & INSPIRATIONAL BOOKS

– an imprint of –

Acclaim Press
— Your Next Great Book —

P.O. Box 238
Morley, MO 63767
(573) 472-9800
www.acclaimpress.com

Book Design: Steward & Wise Graphic Design
Cover Design: Frene Melton

ISBN: 978-1-965370-06-3 | 1-965370-06-3
Library of Congress Control Number: 2025930057
First Printing 2025
Printed in the United States of America
10 9 8 7 6 5 4 3 2 1

This publication was produced using available information.
The publisher regrets it cannot assume responsibility for errors or omissions.

Publications by Dr. Joël Hilaire

On The Other Side Of The Desk – a true story on patients dealing with cancer.
Fantaisie De Ma Jeunesse – poetry in French
Ye Are The Body Of Christ - a medico - theological book
Gemstone – poetry
The Silent Song – poetry
Melody For Claire - poetry

CONTENTS

Introduction 8
Acknowledgements 10
Reserved For the Master's Use 11

THE PROCESS

The Butterfly 18
Follow Him 19
The Bruising Process 20
Sometimes 21
The Overcomer's Journey 23
Sublimation 24
Jesus Understands 25
The Pathway of Suffering 26
Dancing in the Rain 28
Dancing in the Fire 29

SELF - HELP

Inner Thoughts 34
The Impromptu 35
The Essential 36
After All 37
Confidence 39
Dreams 40
Insomnia 42
The Daily Walk 44
Daily Choice 45
Kindness 46
Altruism 47
How to be Bright Stars 49
The Search 51
Inner Strength 52

PRAYER AND MEDITATION

To You Only, Lord 58
Light My Candle 60
The Priceless Reward 61
My Supplication 62
O Abba! 64
Prayer 65
As a Stranger 67
A Ray of Light 68
One Thing 69
Heal My Heart 70
Let Us Pray 71
Prayer Is Powerful 72
A New Dawn 73
Inspiration 74
Calling and Dedication 75

ENDLESS MORNING

The Morning Bliss 82
Farewell 83
Full Circle 85
A Constant Instant Present 86
Joy Comes In The Morning 87
One Day 88
Sweet Fragrance 90
The Right Pathway 91
Where Light Forever Flows 92
About the Author 94

Introduction

Moving Toward Higher Ground completes a trilogy started with two previous publications in poetry: *Gemstone* and *The Silent Song*. Those three books present to the readers a spiritual journey where they can detect a constant progress toward a destination. This destination consists in reaching the highest level in our spiritual walk where, through daily devotion and meditation, we can enjoy peace and be content no matter what can come on our way. Even if it includes serious illness of loved ones or the time they take their last breath. Nature itself teaches us that the sun does not shine every day. Who by now has not experienced cloudy and rainy days, stormy weather, snowy days and nights, tornadoes, hurricanes, or earthquakes, or even a wicked tsunami?

Yet amid all of this, one can experience a real peace that surpasses all understanding. For if you know Him and have entertained a steady relationship with the prince of peace, have no fear. He promised that He would keep in perfect peace whose mind has stayed on Him. It is no secret that we are living in a life full of challenges every day. Those challenges are designed to shape and mold us, and to bring out of us the gemstone hidden deep within. They can make or break us. They can be used as steppingstones or simply become stumbling blocks. It all depends on our responses to those challenges. This journey started in *Gemstone*, a combination of poetry and five short stories to continue in *The Silent Song*.

The Silent Song deeply works on our spirit, to change the bad habits of complaining, murmuring, or fussing into the healthy ones of praising and thanking the Lord while waiting in silence for his salvation. It is hard to study to simply be quiet as mentioned in the writings of the apostle Paul in the Bible. However, this denotes a great level of maturity. Attitudes talk louder than words. The right attitude coupled with a quiet and meek spirit is a powerful tool that can force people around us to think, and to inspire them to change their approach to the things of life. *The Silent Song* opens the door for the need to deeper search in self or introspection. It helps us realize that there are higher heights to climb up to, and deeper depths to explore. This has led to the writing of *Moving Toward Higher Ground*.

Moving Toward Higher Ground is a combination of reflections during hardships, introspection, prayer, and meditation in a quest for real spirituality and a faithful walk with The Master. This handful of poems subdivided into some specific categories can touch and soften the heart, appeal to the mind, and inspire the soul to change. It brings purpose to this current life, offers valuable insights on how to improve self and gives hope for a better tomorrow when our course here is over. It is at times difficult to choose one poem over another as each one seems to teach a specific lesson; each one seems to pull the reader in one direction: keep climbing toward higher ground!

Moving Toward Higher Ground is a special love letter written with one person in mind: YOU, the reader! Once you open it, you will feel like reading it over and over. You might even find yourself saying at times:

Please, let my heart's meditation,
My praise and my adoration
Find favor in your holy sight!

As I submit my life each day
Both to your will and to your way,
Let me become a ray of light.

Joël Hilaire

Acknowledgments

Special thanks to my beautiful and precious wife Claire Edith who brightens my life every day with her presence. I'm so grateful for God's amazing grace toward us.

Special thanks to Dr. Marie Claire Dorismond Adrien for her editing support. Special thanks go as well to Sheila Laguerre for some technical support.

May the Lord bless you all and give you day by day a clearer vision for the things of the Kingdom of God.

Reserved For The Master's Use

Just a simple man, – at times intimidating,
On whom God has called for a purpose.
Eloquently the Scriptures he can expand,
Loving his works with God's great people.

Humility is written all over him,
In deeds as well as in his words.
Leading with such a charisma,
Allowing all around him to be a part,
Introvert, he is, with a big open heart.
Reserved himself only for the Master's use,
Energetic he is, while singing a Silent Song.

Marsha Bethel

Moving Toward Higher Ground

The Process

Life is a journey and is not without a purpose. During this journey from point A to Z, different people experience low points that should inspire them to get into themselves and bring the best out of themselves. Some do and they later share what is considered a "process" in their lives. Unfortunately, some others get discouraged and never bounced back. But every ascension in life comes after a certain process designed to mold, shape, and transform one into what he was supposed to be. Once one can understand that concept, he learns to go through the different phases or stages until he reaches fulfillment or what is known as perfection or full maturity. One analogy I could use to illustrate my point of view is the transformation of a caterpillar into a beautiful, colorful, and joyful butterfly. Observing a butterfly happily flying around is one of the most amusing spectacles one can witness. This analogy can teach so many lessons, knowing that delicate and colorful creature was not always so attractive and delightful to the eyes. It had to go through a process called metamorphosis. What is metamorphosis? How does it occur? How long does it last?

A simple definition for the word metamorphosis from the dictionary is the process of transformation from an immature to an adult form in two or more distinct stages. In the case of a butterfly that metamorphosis goes through four stages at least, depending on the species. It covers a period of 28 to 32 days. Those four stages consist of the egg, the larva, the pupa or chrysalis, then the adult form. Each stage has a function to perform. For example, the caterpillar needs to eat a lot for growth while the adult form needs to reproduce to perpetuate the life cycle of the butterflies.

The first stage of the process starts with a very small oval, round or cylindrical egg depending on the species of the butterfly. When the larva or caterpillar emerges from that egg, this is called the second stage. It can take between four days to three weeks for the egg to hatch. The caterpillar must grow quickly. Therefore, it eats continually before leading to the third stage of the metamorphosis.

Many events occur during the third stage called chrysalis or pupa. That is when the caterpillar (especially molt caterpillar) forms the cocoon which is a silk casing usually brown or green so it can camouflage. During that transformational stage, the caterpillar starts growing wings. Its old body dies, and a new body takes shape inside a protective shell known as chrysalis. A hormone called ecdysone is released to facilitate the whole process when the caterpillar has outgrown its current skin. Inside this cocoon or chrysalis – depending on the species – the caterpillar is completely transformed into a new creature. Ten to fourteen days after the duration of the third stage, the chrysalis becomes transparent, revealing inside a magnificent new creature: the butterfly!

This leads to the final stage of the process, the adult form which will emerge once the chrysalis is completely transparent. The butterfly, so fun to watch happily flying around, will have one important responsibility: reproducing to maintain the life cycle of its species.

With this analogy in mind, I hope the readers can appreciate and feel enlightened as they explore the next few pages of *Moving Toward Higher Ground*. Enjoy!

The Butterfly

I sent you a butterfly
Utterly to help you smile
Even for a little while
So, friend, you won't need to cry.

Butterflies are messengers,
Messengers that bring us hope
While teaching us how to cope
With this life many dangers.

Butterflies are so fragile
Yet everywhere they abound,
Flying well above the ground
No matter how they may feel.

Life can be such a downer
When the least you expect it,
So low dragging your spirit
That you could drown in despair.

Please, receive this butterfly,
A token of my friendship,
A symbol for you to keep
So, you can smile and fly high.

Follow Him

Peter left on the side his boat,
And all his nets, but kept his coat
When he opted to follow Him,
The one with power to redeem.

Matthew also changed his career
To the great surprise of his peers
When came the man of Galilee
Who simply told him: follow me!

Paul, rabbi - to - be from Tarsus,
While on the way to Damascus,
Was, by a light, brought to his knees
Till he could say, "Lord, please, use me!"

They all learned the Lord to follow,
His way and his name to hallow
As in Him they became rooted,
From filthiness separated.

Can you today follow Him too,
No matter what you may go through?
Listen. He is calling your name!
His Word He wants you to proclaim.

The Bruising Process

In the past I used to ask, "Why?"
Each time I had to face a trial.
But since my mind God has opened
On all that to Jesus happened,
I am learning to find his will
On what it takes the flesh to kill.

It pleased the Lord to bruise Jesus.
It will be just the same for us.
He was put to grief and suffering,
Obeyed through prayers and crying.
He kept himself from murmuring,
An example for us leaving.

He's the Potter and we're the clay.
Only by his rules we should play.
He will cover us with his grace
As he'll push us through the furnace.
Unless he molds and shapes us well,
We won't be one of his angels.

Once I understood this process,
I've longed to have Jesus' meekness.
I might have to go through some flood
Or maybe also to sweat blood.
Please, don't let me fail, o my Lord.
Hold me with the strength of your Word.

Sometimes

Sometimes in this journey you're in,
You can feel like a broken doll.
And you know way down deep within
You wish that you could have control
Over the waves swirling around,
Or the earthquakes shaking your ground.

Sometimes it looks as no one cares,
While you're struggling on your own way.
And life does not always seem fair
Regardless how your share you pay.
That is when you must hold on tight
As you know you are in a fight.

Sometimes you can't help asking why
You must go down in the valleys.
Why do you suffer pain and cry?
Why does life bring you on your knees?
You already know the answer
Yet it hits hard as a cancer.

Sometimes you feel like giving up
And simply flying far away.
But you must drink, drink from that cup
To subdue this body of clay.
Then you will sing this brand new song,
Known only by those who stood strong.

This life may not always seem fair
When you must face some grief and pain.
But as soft music fills the air,
Or on the ground falls cooling rain,
Likewise, God has ways to comfort
And lead his children á bon port.

It can be in a still small voice,
Or in a vision of the night.
He knows how your heart to rejoice
As you move closer to his light.
In the eyes of little children,
In a kind word from an old friend …

In the majesty of the sky,
In the splendor of a sunrise,
In the colorful butterfly,
In the ants tiny yet so wise,
God, to us all, talks every day…
We simply ought to learn his ways.

The Overcomer's Journey

From the rugged cross to the crown
From the pit of sin to glory
One can't afford to let self - down
But must fight to walk steadily.

This implies a learning process
To generate pure obedience,
Deny all sort of selfishness,
And let, with kindness, grow patience.

Who can rejoice when facing trials?
Who can be thankful when hurting?
How can one just accept betrayal,
Mainly from those he's been helping?

Where can one even find the strength
To keep climbing the rough mountain?
How can one push fear at arm length
When must one deal with so much pain?

To become an overcomer
Requires more than lips service.
One as clay must trust the Potter
To guide him through his catharsis.

The way to victory and glory
Goes through sacrifice and duress.
To reach purity and beauty
Gold must go through refining first.

So, one must endure till the end
In the quest for eternity.
With sin one no longer can blend
As he's tasted divinity.

Sublimation

There is no gain without pain,
Ascension sans crucifixion.
No need to cry or to complain
Nor fall into a depression.

Simply as a caterpillar
Which coils itself in a cocoon
And without any fanfare
Goes through a deep transformation

To become some nice butterfly
Which delights nature and the eyes,
One can also go in prayers,
Silence and deep meditation

When dealing with this life's affairs
To answer with sublimation.
I know well that hurts and sufferings
Are parts of this journey on earth.

I also know that morning brings
Hope with sunrise … peace with its birth.
So silently on this pathway,
I shall continue my journey,
Keeping always the goal in sight
Until I ascend to the Light.

Jesus Understands

Hung between the earth and heaven
On a cross as a cursed being,
Betrayed and denied by his friends
To whom he vested his teachings,
Detached from Mary, his mother,
Despised, rejected by his own,
Jesus reached out to his Father
As he was feeling so alone.

Surely, he would find some solace
In the One who'd begotten him.
He knew well the amazing grace
They shared before as Elohim!
But as the perfect sacrifice
He was this time covered with sin
And discovered to his surprise
On his Father, he could not lean.

Sensing the depth of his despair,
The coldness of his loneliness
As a thunder tearing the air
His voice revealed his whole distress
When all could hear him shout:
"Eli! Eli Lama sabachthani?"
Hebrew words for: "My God, My God
Why? Why have you forsaken me?"

If Jesus - Christ while on this sod
Could feel so troubled on that day,
How so much more for us today
Living in this house of clay?
I won't say much of my distress,
The hurt from some sounding silence,
But on this way of loneliness,
I know my Jesus understands.

The Pathway Of Suffering

I am no stranger to suffering
As that's also part of living.
It's such a way to discover
If you are better or bitter.

Through fire go silver and gold
Before being shaped in a mold.
Likewise human souls must suffer
To reveal their true character.

Do you know the same hot water
That makes some vegetables softer
Gets from coffee a sweet fragrance
While a fragile egg it hardens?

I know anyone can suffer
Wherever and for whatever.
But how many can still be kind
When tests and trials tickle their mind?

I am aspiring to greatness
And yet that starts with humbleness.
He who wants to be a leader
First must be a good follower.

Now when tests and trials come my way
I am learning to simply say,
"Lord, give me the strength and the grace
To faithfully finish this race."

So instead of being whiners
Let's learn how to become winners.
Suffering is not a punishment
But a tool toward fulfillment.

When one suffers for a just cause,
As the sweet perfume of a rose
Embalms the air when it is smashed
Such should his spirit be when crushed.

If one suffers for his meanness
That's the fruit of his evilness.
But one should display majesty
When tried for his integrity.

So, the pathway toward suffering
Can in us reveal many things.
The way to know you reach greatness
Is when from you it brings kindness.

Dancing In The Rain

Dancing in the rain
At a sweet refrain,
Washing away fear
While hiding my tears.
Life is beautiful
When one sees half – full
The half - empty cup!

I do love the rain
And its sweet refrain
Falling drop by drop
To bury my pain.
Life is beautiful
And you're wonderful!

Though at times stressful,
My life's beautiful ...
God is powerful
To change what's awful
In things meaningful.

He sends me the rain
With its sweet refrain
To melt all my pain
And fill me again
With joy pure and plain.

Dancing in the rain
Is for me such gain.
Life is beautiful
God is powerful!

Dancing In The Fire

Dancing in the fire
And swallowing the heat
Can trigger some ire
In those who cannot fit.

One might covet to talk
To express some feelings,
But one must walk the talk
To accomplish great things.

I have banged at your door
To catch your attention
But with my hands so sore
What's left is illusion.

I have played my music
To appeal to your ears,
But I guess my lyric
Is not easy to hear.

Now a fire is lit
Hotter by the moment,
Blistering certain feet,
Causing astonishment.

But whether in the rain
Or in a bright fire,
One needs to be well trained
To keep rising higher.

While dancing in fire,
May all the slags be burned.
For one to shine brighter,
One must first be well churned.

Self-Help

Man is the result of his genetics, his environment and his training in life. Genetics represents a combination of traits a person inherits through his genes from his parents and even his grandparents. This will determine his appearance (as color of skin, color of his eyes, facial features), his health (with transmission of some diseases as cancer, sickle cell anemia, high blood pressure, etc....) and some other characteristics including natural talents, mental abilities, temperament, etc....). Man's temperament is made of strengths and weaknesses. Surely, he cannot change his genetics but can work on his temperament to maintain his strengths and improve his weaknesses. His environment and training in life, however, are constantly changing. Therefore he feels a need to constantly readjust himself to fit in and project the best of him. This is what we will call self-improvement. The autodidacts could tell us a lot about that.

A wise man said one day, "Be not deceived: evil communications corrupt good manners". There's a saying, "Birds of a feather flock together ... until the cat comes". Our environment has a way to influence us and define who we are. Therefore we must be conscious of who we allow to be in our inner circle. Sometimes to remain true to self and maintain honesty and integrity, we must let go of some acquaintances or simply change our immediate environment. A true leader is like an eagle. If need be, he is not afraid to fly high and alone to set the right example. How do you know you are in the right environment?

The answer is simple: when it inspires you to bring the best out of yourself, stimulates you to keep on striving for the best and allows you to blossom spiritually, morally, intellectually, psychologically, and even financially. Such environment helps you to aspire to what is excellent. Note that financial growth does not necessarily mean that you are evolving in the right environment as such growth can occur through corruption and/or illegal activities such as recreational drug transactions.

The third factor in man outcome is his training in life. This training starts from the crib and continues throughout life. The mind and the heart grab anything they can from parents, relatives, Sunday school teachers, peers in school, colleagues, coworkers, personal reading, and traveling. Someone said, "Tell me what you read, and I will tell you what you are worth". All this influences our character and personality, and how we act and connect with our environment. Learning and training in life are an on-going process.

Overall three words characterize who we are: temperament, personality, and character. Through them we interact with each other and relate to our environment. All three can be improved and help us be better human beings. Our temperaments, which can cause us to be introvert or extrovert (made of strengths and weaknesses) can't be changed but our weaknesses can be worked on to improve who we are while we learn to cultivate our strengths. Our personality is what we display and allow others to see. A charismatic personality can attract people to us and facilitate our connections with others. Our character is how we are when no one is watching. In other words it's the real us, charismatic or not. We're no longer under the light of the projectors, we're not wired to any microphone, we are not performing. When our character and personality match i.e. when we remain the same whether people are observing us or not, then we know that we are real, honest and a person of great integrity. Otherwise, we need to keep on endeavoring to improve ourselves, whether through good reading, counseling, meditation and specialized training for areas in our lives where we need help.

May this section of *Moving Toward Higher Ground* inspire our readers into fulfilling the goal of bringing the best out of themselves each day!

Inner Thoughts

I live every day in my shell,
Away from noise and harmful touch,
And I wonder what I could tell
To let others feel I care much.

I walk every day all alone.
Yet I like the sweetness within.
Under the hardness of a stone
May be found the coolest fountain.

I admire children's innocence,
Which helps them enjoy life's beauty.
Just to find self in their presence,
Gives more sense to simplicity.

I love the rainbow in the sky.
I delight in sounds of nature.
I dream when I see the birds fly.
That brings such hope for the future.

The Impromptu

You seem to forget who I am
And seem to ignore how I feel
After that door you coldly slammed,
And closed your ears to my appeal.

I wish you could say what went wrong
And let me know where I have failed.
My faith in you has been so strong,
I thought on all tests we'd prevail.

I still can hear your clear laughter.
I still can see right through your soul.
I still can feel your soft fingers …
Our lives appeared under control!

Then as a war in time of peace
Or some lightning in a blue sky,
I fell victim of a caprice
And I was dismissed as a fly.

Can you soften your heart again
And reach out toward my hand?
You can easily stop the pain:
Just remember I am your friend.

The Essential

I want to learn the essential,
Leave aside the superficial,
Any mask or anything fake
That triggers the same old mistakes.

Some dive so much in the social,
Tangled in the emotional,
They can miss what is important,
As an inadvertent student.

The essential cannot be seen
With anybody's naked eyes.
The essential is deep within.
It helps the simples become wise.

The essential lasts forever.
With the heart it is discovered.
One can feel so empty and lost
As one neglects what matters most.

I want to find the essential
To climb toward the spiritual.
I said no to the miry clay
Since I have found heaven's highway.

After All

I am the shadow on the wall
That has caught no one attention.
I am the candid voice that calls,
But finds no caring reception.

I am somewhat a pleasant book
Full inside with great instructions.
But really no one cares to look,
Obsessed with one's own condition.

In this life people never learn
How well they should treat each other.
But at the point of no return
They get their big eye opener.

Why do we offer nice flowers,
When one can no longer see them?
Why do we cry like a river,
When one goes to "Mathusalem"?

I wish to be shown great esteem,
When it could still brighten my day.
I want to be part of one's team
And be cheered now along the way.

We hurt with words when one can hear
And say nice things when it's too late.
We cause people to live in fear,
And fail to them kindly relate.

What has happened to compassion,
Gentleness, patience and kindness?
Since when for our main emotions
We show meanness and selfishness?

What becomes of the golden rule,
Which says to do unto others
What to us would be nice and cool?
In fact, aren't we all brothers?

I may be shadow on the wall,
Or a faint voice that is calling
But someone loves me after all
And keeps me each day from falling.

Confidence

I can't tell you about the weights
That I am carrying inside.
You already have your full plate.
I long here to enjoy my ride.
So, I humbly ask help me pray
That nothing can pull me astray.

Do not get me wrong in thinking
I'm trying to hide anything.
To lean on Jesus, I'm learning.
So, I put aside complaining
As I've been taught in everything,
I must say thank you to the King.

Murmuring, fussing, complaining
Rob us the strength from rejoicing.
Praying, praising and worshipping
Help build a strong bond with the Lord
And develop love for his Word,
Which is to us a useful sword.

Listen, I'm in this race to stay
As I walk in this narrow way.
I want to put aside all weight
And upon the Lord learn to wait.
Life to me now is so pleasing,
Since I got rid of complaining.

Dreams

Anyone who no longer dreams,
Chooses also to stop living.
He becomes like a ghost strolling
Aimlessly in the spirit realm.

Dreams give a certain sense to life:
Some will rejuvenate the heart.
Others propel you in a strife,
And keep you from falling apart.

Some dreams can seem impossible
Yet bring out the best from your soul.
What to some seems not feasible
Can lead you to a pot of gold.

What one needs is not dream crushers
To make one feel just like a fool
But instead, some great cheerleaders
To change all bumps in useful tools.

I dream each day of a new earth
Where there will be no more hatred.
And when we get such a rebirth,
This life to us will be sacred!

There will be no need for weapons
For we'll live in such harmony.
No fear of an Armageddon
As we'll sing a love symphony!

Children will not starve anymore
But in green pastures will delight.
We won't judge people by color
For we'll be all children of light.

Why having discrimination
Over so many petty things?
Since when hatred and divisions
Were tools for peace and rejoicing?

I long to run in open fields
Where bloom all colorful flowers.
I want to see playgrounds well built
Where can be heard songs and laughter.

I love great and beautiful lakes
Where friends come and build souvenirs,
Or lovers stroll to take a break
In such a serene atmosphere!

I think of some of my old dreams.
Some still bring a smirk on my face.
Others are not worth to redeem
And yet could make my old heart race.

Listen, don't quash my dreams away!
Though for you they might be senseless,
They keep me going day by day
And remind me that I am blessed!

Insomnia

Why at night now is my sleep gone,
Leaving me awake and alone
With those deep thoughts and those feelings
That more turmoil and unrest bring?

The nights appear to be longer.
The thoughts come from so much deeper.
Some are gentle and inspiring.
Others, not so kind and troubling.

It is shocking to discover
Such thoughts and feelings were still there.
One must uproot carnality
To rebuild the mind's purity.

In order to eliminate
What's known as the unconscious mind,
One must for sure eradicate
All things unseemly or unkind.

I need the Word in my whole mind,
From conscious to the unconscious.
Then I will no longer be blind
To what for me is so precious.

I am longing for a pure heart
All the way down to my "qerev." *
The mind is just the outside part
Inside starts with "beten" ** and "lev." ***

As was for the tables of law
Written on both parts of their sides,
So must it be today also:
The mind and the heart are the sides.

The Word can be found in the mind,
Which represents the outside.
In the heart it must be hidden:
That's when it is written inside.

When tests and trials on the way come
They really tell what we're made of.
Each time we fail to overcome,
We know we are still in the rough.

So now I know if I can't sleep
There's some special work to be done.
I need to dig a little deep
And be sure that those thoughts are gone!

*Qerev: the heart or the mind as the seat of thought and desire. (Psalms 5:9; Psalms 49:11; Psalms 64:6). It is also the seat of laughter. (Genesis 18:12)

**Beten: the inmost part, the bottom of the heart, the inward parts of the belly. (Proverbs 20:27).

***Lev: the heart, the inner part of a thing. It is considered as the seat of the will. (Numbers 16:28; Judges 9:3; I Chronicles 12:14). It is also the seat of moral evil. (Jeremiah 17:9).

Qerev, beten and lev are Hebrew words used in the Old Testament in relationship with the heart.

The Daily Walk

I walked along the way today
Hoping a glimpse of you to gain
But I must have missed your pathway
As I looked all around in vain.

Walking around every morning
Has become to me daily bread.
That has helped my inner being
In a righteous path to be led.

It starts my day on the right note
With prayer and meditation.
It gives me strength not to be caught
In the snares of my temptations.

I want each day to grow stronger
To do the right and shone the wrong.
Your Word can make my path brighter
And cause me to sing a new song.

Along the way, I'll walk again
Day after day, circumspectly
Hoping a glimpse of you to gain
To help me do all things justly.

Daily Choice

For you here's a sweet melody
To sing, rejoice, and celebrate.
Laughter is such a remedy!
No need to go around irate.

For me, each day is a blessing.
I can learn more in life and grow.
It is such a beautiful thing
When, in one, wisdom and joy flow.

Your life can be a symphony,
A blend of divine harmony
If you trust in the Almighty.

My life is such a great journey
Where I no longer have my way
But trusting in Him greatly pays.

Kindness

Kindness has a way to travel
And touch another person's life!
It can also help untangle
The complexities of one's strife...

It might take a simple gesture
Carried out innocently.
Yet when placed in a great picture,
It can change one's life completely.

And what makes it so beautiful,
Kindness is just its own reward!
So simple and yet powerful
As through it, faith can be restored.

One may not have even perceived
The rippling effect of his deeds
But those who were there to receive
Will not surely fail to take heed.

An act of kindness is priceless,
As it marks the heart forever.
It blesses the soul in distress,
Hope and comfort it can offer.

Never hesitate to be kind.
It is not a sign of weakness.
It's the pathway to help one find
The majesty of selflessness.

Altruism

I am at times scared of silence
But I panic at your silence.
Because I long for affection,
I feel hurt by your rejection.

I wish you were a mind reader,
My inner thoughts to decipher.
My bare feelings you can't detect,
Why, such from you, should I expect?

This rough journey I did not choose,
But some weights I got to let loose.
Bitterness and no forgiveness
Can keep anybody oppressed.

But free as a bird in the sky
I want to be able to fly.
I long to sing meaningful songs
That can cause others to feel strong.

Maybe alone should I travel
To be at peace and to excel?
Or should I learn to be content
With what I see in this instant?

Wisdom wants me to be careful
As life at times can be awful.
Great lessons I can still attain,
Whether it is sunshine or rain.

I surely cannot overcome
Those things in life that make me numb
If I keep on running away
Each time hardships come on my way.

So, I must face the cold silence
And, from its sound, learn how to dance.
I must stare at vile rejection
To connect with my heart's passion.

Beauty can be born from ashes
And peace emanates from clashes.
Buried talents can come to light
As one learns to master his fright.

So, my heart, get ready to sing
And to others be a blessing.
As an eagle you can fly high
No matter how may look the sky.

How To Be Bright Stars

Into the garden of your heart,
You invited me for a walk.
You wanted me to be a part,
You told me during our talk.

You show me a nice flowerbed
Where you grow trust and tenderness.
Where used to be wrath and hatred,
Now blossom patience and kindness.

I saw a bench under a tree.
You call it the bench of friendship.
It helps your mind to become free,
When you must deal with some hardship.

Next to it was the strangest bush
That I wanted to examine.
You gave my hand a gentle push
Away from that bush dry and green.

"Don't!" You said with a nervous laugh.
"The green portion is forgiveness,
The dry part which is sharp and rough
Symbolizes forgetfulness."

"When I am exposed to meanness,
I find refuge on bench friendship.
Fighting to avoid bitterness,
I throw in this bush all bad chips...."

"When I forget, they become dry.
When I forgive, they can turn green.
And touching them can make me cry
As it'll bring back the hurtful scenes."

With time, I hope all becomes green,
And my place, a true paradise.
Sometimes the ugly face of sin
Tries to trick me through some disguise.

Then weeds grow all over the place.
If out I'm not quick to pull them,
They rob me from His precious grace,
Causing me to feel all ashamed."

The garden of your heart looked neat
Pleasant to my sight and my smell.
The mixture of freshness and heat
Made me feel like under a spell.

The fruit trees and the nice flowers
Reflect your personality.
They show also your character,
Your wit and your integrity.

I looked around and felt at ease,
Pleased by your trust and openness.
The air was moved by a cool breeze
That surrounds the soul with calmness.

I turned toward your trusting face
And felt a wave of gentleness.
My eyes, your whole garden, embrace
Filled with a sense of awesomeness.

Choosing to leave on people's heart
Kind footprints and not ugly scars
Is as beautiful as the art
Of knowing how to be bright stars.

The Search

Searching for a new home to stay
Can be like peeling a cabbage.
Each time you miss the one you prey,
Nicer ones come on your passage.

It can be such an adventure
Requiring good faith and patience.
When each try ends up in failure,
Don't let it become a nuisance.

For you, there must be a sure place
Like you are dreaming in your heart,
And where you will find your solace.

Remember God always knows best,
And when you should have a fresh start.
For this too can be just a test.

Inner Strength

One day I walked along the sea,
Searching for peace and harmony,
Leaving behind for a moment
The wild city and its torment.

How pleasant to see the water
And bask in its healing power!
Somehow it freed me from life's toll
And seemed to help me soothe my soul.

Suddenly my mind felt so clear
And my inner self I could hear...
My heart's eyes became wide open
As my feet relaxed in the sand.

What was that consuming feeling
Enveloping my whole being,
Galvanizing me all over
As the wind made me feel cooler?

Why was I now finding new thought
For what all my life I have fought
In my quest for true happiness
To prevent me from emptiness?

For long, people and circumstance,
I thought, would bring me my credence
And I would sink into sadness,
If I were to face their meanness.

But now like a sweet melody
As the wind caressed my body
I could hear in me a kind voice
Telling me that I had a choice.

"You choose to be happy or sad,
To be content or to be mad.
We all possess an inner strength
That carries us through any length.

You remain the sole architect
Of what in life you could expect.
You only can alter the lines
Once you've completed your design."

My lips then parted in a smile
As I savored a little while
The deep meaning of my finding,
Which made me feel much like shouting!

A burden fell off my shoulders
And my pace became much faster.
The calm water soothed my soul.
Oh, how have I enjoyed my stroll!

Prayer and Meditation

Prayer, a mystery for many people but a reality for others. It's a way of communicating with God whether some want to admit it or not. This has been so puzzling that with the invention of MRI and CT scan, a group of researchers in neuroscience decided to conduct a few studies on the matter. The conclusion reached by the scientists is that prayer is real, and it affects the central nervous system in lighting up certain areas in the brain of those who faithfully pray and meditate. It works even from a distance and carries with it the power of healing. It can change people's disposition and soften their hearts. In that case what can we say about prayer?

A simple definition of prayer is a conversation with God for a specific request, a petition, or simply a way of entertaining a good relationship with the Heavenly Father. Based on the needs, one can address all types of prayers to the Lord: worship, confession, supplication, intercession, deliverance, thankfulness, prayer of faith, prayer of consecration and even prayer of the Holy Spirit That prayer of the Holy Spirit is when we don't know what to pray for and yet we moan and groan before the Lord in our spirit. It is not my intention to make an exhaustive study of the topic here. So many titles on this great subject can be found on the market. I simply want to use those few words to introduce this section of *Moving Toward Higher Ground*.

May the texts under this heading inspire the readers to develop their own prayer lives, to find time for meditation, and consecration. One point of importance is that those who live a life of prayer and meditation have a certain aura around them that others can sense, and which confers on them a spiritual authority that is difficult to explain. The truth is they seem to have a connection with higher spiritual powers and a protection that even themselves can't explain.

A sincere life of prayer brings with it a strong desire to practice what is right, peace of mind, and a sense of being content no matter what comes one's way. People who pray faithfully do not feel overwhelmed by the circumstances of life, but they seem to always have a sense of hope even in dire situations. They don't easily give up in the face of adversity. Their presence among their peers brings a sense of strength and stability. Prayer is powerful. It lightens up the spirit, soothes the disposition and relaxes the soul …

To You Only, Lord

To you only let my life be
A true and living sacrifice.
Let me each day get rid of me
And my soul may no lust entice.

Why should I still, Lord, to you bring
Any trespass or sin offering?
Why can't I delight in your laws
So, I can erase all my flaws?

My life can be a burnt offering
Holy, in very good standard,
Consumed into ashes to bring
Underneath the incense altar.

I can come with a meat offering
With frankincense as your Spirit,
And oil as good understanding
Without omitting salt in it.

I will not add any leaven,
A type of falsehood or malice.
How can I walk toward heaven
With in me any prejudice?

I'm not to add any honey,
A product of my carnal mind.
So, I learn to stay on my knee
Till clearly your will I can find.

You've been so good to me, my Lord.
How can I help but be thankful?
So much strength I find in your Word!
I can feel that my cup is full.

My heart desire is to bring,
Whenever I come toward you,
A pure drink and good peace offering,
A way to express my love too.

To you only, Lord, I belong.
Teach me how with you to walk right.
I want gracefully to sing your song
And let through me shine your bright light.

Light My Candle

Light my candle, o Lord my God
So, I may shine before your throne.
Your name I proclaim on this sod
As I am no longer my own.

You have shown me grace and mercy.
You are teaching me uprightness.
My eyes now you allow to see
As you have pulled me from darkness.

My feet you make strong every day
So, I can follow in your footsteps.
I discovered in this pathway
I can't afford any misstep.

I love the shield of salvation.
I hide in you, my high tower,
As I am fighting those nations.
You are my strength and my buckler.

Why would I fail to overcome
The tests and trials of every day
When I know well what is to come
If in this way I choose to stay?

I long to dwell in your presence
Where there is joy for evermore.
At the light of your countenance,
My soul finds delight more and more.

The Priceless Reward

Your majesty has no likeness.
Awesome is your loving kindness.
You know how to use graciousness
To inspire the powerless!

In your presence one is speechless,
Feeling so crushed by your greatness
Meanwhile you are all gentleness,
If one may say in all fairness.

He who can walk in righteousness
And delight in your holiness
Knows well what it means to be blessed
And be somewhat free of distress.

To such a one you're a fortress:
He can journey through life fearless.
On his pathway lies true success
As to you, now, he has access.

Running this race with humbleness,
Toward the high mark one should press.
One really cannot hope for less,
Once by your grace one has been blessed.

O in white linen to be dressed,
Is worth going through the process
That leads toward the hot furnace!
To be like YOU is just priceless!

My Supplication

O Lord, hear my supplication
And look at my situation.
You are my refuge, my portion,
While facing those seven nations.

You see all my persecutions,
As well as my heart's volition.
I lean not on my reactions,
But rely on your compassion.

Your will for me is perfection.
Let me reach such expectation.
You have made me good provision,
So, I can maintain my vision.

Your Holy Word brings salvation,
Your Holy Ghost, consolation.
Your shepherds give good instructions
To guide me through all my options.

My mind needs deep transformation.
My heart longs for true conversion.
My conscience wants the right pulsion
So, I can climb up mount Zion.

O Lord, hear my supplication
For pure temple adoration.
Living in sanctification
Can lead me toward perfection.

It can bring such satisfaction
To know I've quelled all temptations,
And met all your expectations …
You are my strength and my portion.
My Lord, hear my supplication.

O Abba!

O Father of the creation,
You have all my admiration.
All your works are pure perfection
And great source of inspiration.
To you I bow in submission,
You deserve my adoration.

Let me find favor in your face
As around me abounds your grace.
I know that's not an easy race
If your feet I do not embrace.
This flesh must go through the furnace
So, I can move at your own pace.

Your eyes are so full of kindness.
Your words comfort with gentleness.
Your touch conveys such tenderness.
All this is done in humbleness.
How can one play with filthiness,
Once one tasted your holiness?

To the just you're a strong tower,
A fortress, and a sure buckler.
You're a refuge and a helper
To save us from all destroyers.
Thanks for answering our prayers,
O Abba, Heavenly Father!

Prayer

Lord, the road is so steep,
And I don't want to flip.
Please, here's my hand to keep.
Help me finish this trip.

Father, on you I lean
When all around me spins.
You know well what I mean.
You see me deep within.

To you I bring my pain,
You, the Lamb, for me slain.
No need to all explain,
Nor even to complain.

In you I can have hope.
You teach me how to cope.
You changed water in wine.
You make wrong becomes fine.

In a storm as a ship
Finds refuge in a port,
So, in your flock as sheep
I find in you comfort.

You are source of healing.
You created all things.
Too hard is there a thing,
To naught that you can't bring?

I know you're wonderful.
I know you are skillful.
I know you're all power.
That's why you're The Master.

Here I drop at your feet
What wants to give me fit.
In you there's no defeat.
None with you can compete.

You're the Rock of ages.
You fought on all stages.
You stood all kind of tests.
So, in you lays my rest.

Lord, the road may be steep,
But here's my hand to keep.
I have no more alarms:
I feel safe in your arms.

As A Stranger

As a stranger on a strange land,
I find it at times hard to blend,
Even with my own surroundings
As on this sod I'm traveling.

And yet there's a song I must sing,
Also, good tidings I must bring.
There are great lessons to be learned,
Before to the Lord I return.

As a book in an unlearned hand,
As a deep river through the land
Scaring away the non - swimmers,
I remain simply a stranger.

My voice I am learning to tame.
My flesh I let burn in the flame
Coming from your powerful Word
So, my good tidings can be heard.

O Lord, you know how that feels
As your own, with you, could not deal.
Yet you learn to submit your will
So, your mission could be fulfilled.

As in your footsteps I follow,
Don't let my life, please, be hollow.
Help me endure until the end
While with sin I don't want to blend.

A Ray Of Light

Let it shine, dear Lord, let it shine!
Let your Word each day shine in me.
I want to reach glory divine
And be able your face to see.

Let me, my Lord, sing the new song,
The song of Moses and the Lamb.
With your angels I'll go along
And blend with the heavenly band.

Please, let my heart's meditation,
My praise and my adoration
Find favor in your holy sight!

As I submit my life each day
Both to your will and to your way,
Let me become a ray of light.

One Thing

Many things one can desire
In this world troubled with mire.
Many dreams one can entertain
That may result at times in pain!

But one thing I ask of the Lord
Whom I gladly serve and adore
Is to reside in his presence
Throughout my whole existence

To behold his magnificence
And to admire his beauty!
To me, what a holy duty!

My heart longs after you, o Lord!
Much delight I find in your Word.
Part in your temple let me be.

Heal My Heart

Some things in this life
Come only with time...
We're in such rough strife
That it seems a crime
To 'ven laugh or smile.

Some things nowadays
Pierce the heart so deep
It feels one always
On bleeding will keep
In this endless trial.

And yet God's power
Has known no limit.
He hears all prayers
And through His Spirit,
Can comfort and heal.

So, heal my heart, Lord!
YOU, only, know how.
Your Spirit, your Word
Can easily flow
And fix my vessel.

Heal my broken heart.
Help me hope again.
Let me be a part,
And change this deep pain
In peaceful refrain.

Let Us Pray

You told me a certain morning
Let's keep each other in prayers.
For some that may sound like nothing
As they've never been in despair.

But for me, I can sense a need
To draw to God somewhat closer
So, to this plea, I've taken heed
And here is part of my answer:

Prayer is such a source of strength.
Able to keep us connected.
It helps us stay on same wavelength,
Though physically separated.

Prayer is a food for the soul,
Well able to help us be whole.
Any fortress it can crumble,
While teaching us to be humble.

Prayer is so much more than words.
It's also a protective sword,
An attitude, a state of mind,
Helping the heart to become kind.

When in sincere prayers we sink,
We can discover a strong link
Between you and I and our God
To guide us safely on the road.

As we move on in this journey
Hoping to stay in the right way
So, dear friend, let us really pray,
Relying on the Lord each day!

Prayer Is Powerful

Prayer is powerful
For God is merciful.
He can feel, see and hear
Even our silent tears.

Why bother to complain
For every single pain?
Or why making a scene
And stop being serene?

No matter what happens
The Lord is the captain.
So, a word of prayer

To my blessed Savior
And I know the answer
Will make my life better.

A New Dawn

This life is just like a vapor,
Or like a shadow on a wall.
In a second, he is no more
Who yesterday was standing tall.

And yet today is a new dawn
That I greet with such gratitude.
I can be as a graceful swan,
Charming, with a kind attitude.

Or I can be a complainer,
Finding mistakes in everything.
I could also be a boaster,
Simply going around gloating.

The choice remains mine every day
To be like a ray of sunlight.
So pleasant can be this journey
If I learn not to dim my light.

So, Lord I welcome this new spring,
And another chance to do well
Grant me to fairly keep striving,
Be one of your precious jewels.

Inspiration

Each day creation starts over
With the wonders of the morning!
Always a new set of colors,
Delightful and awe-inspiring!

I can't help thinking how thoughtful
Must be our Heavenly Father
To draw sceneries so wonderful
For all His children anywhere!

I have visited some islands
And many countries in Europe.
He knows the colors how to blend
In all those places to sow hope.

I have explored America
And admired so much beauty.
I've also been to Africa
And seen life in its purity.

Wherever one goes, he can see
Art and beauty from a Master
Who can use heaven, land or sea,
Magnificence to deliver.

Whether it is morning, or night
His awesomeness has no limit.
Whether it's sunlight or starlight,
His majesty we must admit.

And when we're mixed in the picture,
The Masterpiece, more appealing,
Brings more awareness to nature
And makes us feel like worshiping!

Calling And Dedication

His mantle placed on my shoulders,
I have become His follower.
He told me in a still small voice,
"In your heart, make me your first choice."

At first, I didn't quite understand
All that I would have to withstand.
But as I go on this pathway,
He's revealing me all His ways.

I must first learn His righteousness
And move on into holiness.
I keep learning in this journey,
He does not like things done halfway.

Holiness wants separation
From all the wants and the passions.
Called also sanctification,
It surely leads to perfection.

Unless one has the right vision,
This sounds like pure aberration.
The carnal mind can't understand
What pertains to the Holy Land.

What to others appears so cool
Makes one simply look like a fool.
It's not without sacrifice
Anyone can grow in God's eyes.

Take Abraham, Job and Daniel
Or Noah, Moses and Samuel.
For God, all these men took a stand
That many could not understand.

To be called a true Man of God,
Requires wearing His ephod,
And be clothed with the right garments,
While holding all His commandments.

His mantle placed on my shoulders
I have become His prisoner.
I said goodbye to all my dreams.
I live now in another realm.

Endless Morning

One day will come where I will take my last ride in the sunset to enter in what is called the endless morning. I will say farewell to my loved ones and that is fine. It's a predetermined appointment that no one can't miss or escape from. No matter how much one begs, pleads, or cries, it will happen. "To everything there is a season", said King Solomon in his book Ecclesiastes, "and a time to every purpose under the heaven: a time to be born, and a time to die…" The problem is most people seem to forget and are never ready when this time comes. We are sent on earth with a mission and for a preset time. Why are we always so surprised when it is clearly said in the book of Psalms "Your eyes saw my unformed body; all the days ordained for me were written in your book before one of them came to be"?

Knowing this, it is my responsibility to get myself ready so I can enjoy the transition when it comes. Moses himself said in one of his prayers, "So teach us to number our days, that we may apply our hearts unto wisdom". My passport must be in order, my ticket ready and my clothing appropriate. If not, I can end up in the wrong gate and the wrong destination. And I am not referring here to heaven or hell as it's the common belief.

No one is in heaven now, or I must say third heaven, where dwell God the Father and His Son and the hosts of angels at His service, whether cherubim, seraphim, or legions of angels. A selected group of people will make it to third heaven at a specific time for what is called "the marriage supper of the Lamb". This specific group is called the Bride of Christ and is made of 144,000 souls.

There is not a burning place called hell where people are roasted without being ever consumed. This is incompatible with the nature of God who is love. Hell is oblivion for some or the grave for others. In due time, those who are in the grave will come back to life to complete the process of perfection to fit into what is known as the endless morning. This is called resurrection and not reincarnation. The essential is that there is a life after this life and my responsibility is to be ready for it. My purpose is to meet the requirements that allow me to move from one body to another or to have my name inscribed in the Book of life — a prerequisite for resurrection.

This section of *Moving Toward Higher Ground* is much more than just a few poems to read but strong belief on the meaning of eternity and the importance of leaving a sweet fragrance behind long after one takes that last breath and ride freely toward blessed eternity. Don't feel sad but enjoy it! Knowing this brings hope. After all, didn't the great apostle Paul said, "to die is gain"?

The Morning Bliss

I'm looking but I don't see you.
I'm listening but don't hear you.
I'm touching but I don't feel you.
No matter wherever I look,
I cannot see any darkness.

So much harmony! Such brightness!
What is that sound that keeps me hooked?
Is it a divine melody?
Is it the angels' symphony?
I've never seen this place before.

I'm trying to learn more and more.
I've heard about endless morning
But really no words have meaning
To describe what I'm witnessing.
This is a world within a world:
Visible and invisible
Seem to be indivisible.

More and more I feel my head swirling.
To you all I send my last kiss:
I just enter the morning bliss!

Farewell

Listen, I'm not going to lie:
I do not like to say goodbye.
So as the time is drawing near
I might discreetly disappear.

As words engrafted deep in stone
Or muscles attached to a bone,
My heart can get so connected,
I know it would be affected.

So many moments have brought joy!
Moments dear as some precious toys!
Moments that touched me to my core,
Moments considered as treasure!

Laughter is a simple pleasure
But how refreshing to the soul!
A gentle walk into nature:
Such peaceful moment to recall!

Who said that clean life is boring?
Can two hearts be softly beating,
Can two hands meet in gentleness,
Simply because of pure kindness?

Why should some motives be so wrong
To cause some to sing a strange song?
What happened to the innocence
Of a calm and gentle presence?

Life here has been a great journey
Where I 've learned to enjoy each day.
Some days have been bright as a light
Others dark, scary as the night.

A Constant Instant Present

You know, in the land where we were
The time does not really matter.
It's a constant instant present
Where is not found a dull moment.

Some places are somewhat ageless.
Some moments just leave you speechless.
Time and word are irrelevant
In a constant instant present.

You sense much yet nothing can tell,
As you are bound under a spell.
At the door of eternity,
You discover simplicity.

You can bask, glow or you can shine
As if under glory divine
Because there's nothing more pleasant
Than a constant instant present.

Smile and laughter don't fade away.
Kindness is like on the first day.
Only love gets to grow sweeter
As real life now you discover.

Until you can explore such land
You really cannot understand
The splendor and all the sweetness
From two hearts filled with tenderness.

I long for an endless morning
Without pain, grief, and mourning
Love, peace, and joy will fill the air
And time will no longer matter.

Joy Comes In The Morning

As night is the door to daylight
So is death to the afterlife.
Night can bring an unexplained fright.
Death carries anxiety and strife.

Yet someone has called death a gain,
The start of a new beginning
Without hurts, tears, grief and pain,
The door to an endless morning.

Jesus came with resurrection,
A source of hope for tomorrow.
He showed the way to perfection
So, we can move to high from low.

The power of resurrection
Starts with a great deal of suffering
Which ends in the crucifixion.
But joy will come in the morning.

Sweet Fragrance

One day this race will be over
My voice will no longer be heard.
I'll fly away just like a bird
Moving toward the bright summer.

Surely some will remember well
The moments of sweet fellowship,
The warm embrace of true friendship
That kept us close under a spell.

As I travel this path today
It is the time, it is the place
To spread around words filled with grace
That can help others find their way.

Why wouldn't I leave gentle footprints
In the hearts where I was allowed
To dwell safe in time of dark clouds
So, I would not by fear just faint?

And why should not I leave behind
A melody, a sweet fragrance
To fill the void from my absence
For my loved ones and my dear friends?

The day is coming when I'll fly.
A silent song I'll leave behind.
You might well hear it in your mind
Then you'll know I am still close by.

The Right Pathway

I live each day now as my last,
Trusting in God for tomorrow.
The world seems ready for a blast,
One wonders which way one should go.

In just a twinkle of an eye,
Nature wants to regain its rights.
It could be a good time to try
To learn to love and not to fight.

Why not go back to the basics
Of living, loving, and laughing?
Why not relearning how to speak
And appreciate life's little things?

Can one value the essential,
And connect with the inner self?
Can one skip the superficial
And really search for life's true wealth?

I know health, love, and true friendship
Goodness, thoughtfulness, and kindness
Can be just words on certain lips
Nevertheless, they're so priceless!

I want to consider my ways,
And focus on life's true meaning.
It's so easy to go astray,
And to end up out missing.

So, learning to number my days
Has become my priority.
This sets me on the right pathway
Toward a blessed eternity.

Where Light Forever Flows

Behold are coming to an end
All the days of my pilgrimage
On this, at times, tormented land
Where I often felt in bondage.

I got rid of all the luggage
Provided by the carnal mind.
It does require some courage
To leave sin and its joy behind.

At first, I kept in my vessel
The oil caused by understanding.
And as with the flesh I wrestled,
More and more my light kept shining.

I learned to be a reflection
Of the one whose name is the Word.
I put aside all my passions,
And let him in my heart be Lord.

In his footsteps I have followed
So, I can become like the sun,
Source of light above and below,
Producer of life on the ground.

My ascension toward the light
Has led me toward consciousness …
A light so pure, a light so bright
Where words can become so useless.

As crystal are the surroundings.
The soul becomes phosphorescent.
So strong is the sense of being,
One feels in a constant present.

Obsolete become time and space.
No words can describe this new place.
Once of pure light you've been embraced,
Why to darkness would you regress?

I have a glimpse of the future,
And I have tasted tomorrow.
My soul, disregard any stir!
Let's go where light forever flows!

About the Author

When on November 30, 2007, Dr. Joël Hilaire was ordained the pastor of Orlando Gospel Assembly, he opened a brand new chapter in his life. That same day also, he thought that he had closed another section of his life as that marked his last day at the cardiology clinic where he had labored for five years in Tampa, Florida as the assistant of a renowned cardiologist. He didn't realize that from being a caretaker of the human body, he was now going to watch both over the body and the spirit. He was caring for souls. Many people, by curiosity, asked him how can you leave the practice of medicine to pastor in Orlando a small church of about 50 people in a trailer, a church with a tumultuous past with his previous leaderships?

He smiled and simply uttered, "I am answering now to a higher calling in my life!"

It has been 17 years now and a few months. The church has grown spiritually and numerically. The congregation had overgrown the building. He was obligated to change the location. He is working on expanding on their 4 acres of land located on Dean Road at East Orlando. This book is fully dedicated as a fundraising tool for this project. He is assisted in his tasks by a well-trained and devoted staff and the congregation has so beautifully flourished. For many years, he has been the editor in chief of a well maintained newsletter no longer in circulation. Instead, he encouraged the church to have its own website, www.orlandogospelassembly.org. He live-streams the services on YouTube on Wednesdays evening and Sundays afternoon and evening. He maintains a Bible study on zoom every Friday evening from 8:00 pm to 9:30 pm. Two Saturdays a month he visits and encourages via zoom the Cornerstone Assembly located in Nassau, Bahamas - a church of the Body of Christ under the leadership of his Overseer, the Reverend Robert Walker who also pastors his own church at Lakeland, Florida.

Dr. Hilaire enjoys writing and has already published the following works:

On the Other Side of the Desk
Fantaisie de ma Jeunesse
Gemstone
The Silent Song
Ye Are the Body of Christ
Melody for Claire

His current publication, *Moving Toward Higher Ground*, offers to the readers a combination of some choice spiritual poems subdivided in four categories able to touch and soften the heart, appeal to the mind and inspire the soul to change with the ultimate goal to make it to the endless morning.

Dr. Joël Hilaire has been married now for 37 years and continues to care both for his wife (chronically ill for the past 5 years) and his church - the Orlando Gospel Assembly.